The Ghetto and Other Poems

Lola Ridge

Contents

THE GHETTO
AND OTHER POEMS

BY

Lola Ridge

TO THE AMERICAN PEOPLE

Will you feast with me, American People?
But what have I that shall seem good to you!

On my board are bitter apples
And honey served on thorns,
And in my flagons fluid iron,
Hot from the crucibles.

How should such fare entice you!

THE GHETTO

I

Cool, inaccessible air
Is floating in velvety blackness shot with steel-blue lights,
But no breath stirs the heat
Leaning its ponderous bulk upon the Ghetto
And most on Hester street...

The heat...
Nosing in the body's overflow,
Like a beast pressing its great steaming belly close,
Covering all avenues of air...

The heat in Hester street,
Heaped like a dray
With the garbage of the world.

Bodies dangle from the fire escapes
Or sprawl over the stoops...
Upturned faces glimmer pallidly--
Herring-yellow faces, spotted as with a mold,
And moist faces of girls
Like dank white lilies,
And infants' faces with open parched mouths that suck at the air
 as at empty teats.

Young women pass in groups,
Converging to the forums and meeting halls,
Surging indomitable, slow
Through the gross underbrush of heat.
Their heads are uncovered to the stars,
And they call to the young men and to one another
With a free camaraderie.
Only their eyes are ancient and alone...

The street crawls undulant,
Like a river addled
With its hot tide of flesh
That ever thickens.
Heavy surges of flesh
Break over the pavements,
Clavering like a surf--
Flesh of this abiding
Brood of those ancient mothers who saw the dawn break over Egypt...
And turned their cakes upon the dry hot stones
And went on
Till the gold of the Egyptians fell down off their arms...
Fasting and athirst...
And yet on...

Did they vision--with those eyes darkly clear,
That looked the sun in the face and were not blinded--
Across the centuries
The march of their enduring flesh?
Did they hear--
Under the molten silence
Of the desert like a stopped wheel--
(And the scorpions tick-ticking on the sand...)
The infinite procession of those feet?

II

I room at Sodos'--in the little green room that was Bennie's--
With Sadie
And her old father and her mother,
Who is not so old and wears her own hair.

Old Sodos no longer makes saddles.
He has forgotten how.
He has forgotten most things--even Bennie who stays away
 and sends wine on holidays--
And he does not like Sadie's mother
Who hides God's candles,
Nor Sadie
Whose young pagan breath puts out the light--
That should burn always,
Like Aaron's before the Lord.

Time spins like a crazy dial in his brain,
And night by night
I see the love-gesture of his arm
In its green-greasy coat-sleeve
Circling the Book,
And the candles gleaming starkly
On the blotched-paper whiteness of his face,
Like a miswritten psalm...
Night by night
I hear his lifted praise,
Like a broken whinnying
Before the Lord's shut gate.

Sadie dresses in black.
She has black-wet hair full of cold lights
And a fine-drawn face, too white.
All day the power machines
Drone in her ears...
All day the fine dust flies
Till throats are parched and itch
And the heat--like a kept corpse--
Fouls to the last corner.

Then--when needles move more slowly on the cloth
And sweaty fingers slacken
And hair falls in damp wisps over the eyes--
Sped by some power within,
Sadie quivers like a rod...
A thin black piston flying,
One with her machine.

She--who stabs the piece-work with her bitter eye
And bids the girls: "Slow down--
You'll have him cutting us again!"
She--fiery static atom,
Held in place by the fierce pressure all about--
Speeds up the driven wheels
And biting steel--that twice
Has nipped her to the bone.

Nights, she reads
Those books that have most unset thought,
New-poured and malleable,
To which her thought
Leaps fusing at white heat,
Or spits her fire out in some dim manger of a hall,

Or at a protest meeting on the Square,
Her lit eyes kindling the mob...
Or dances madly at a festival.
Each dawn finds her a little whiter,
Though up and keyed to the long day,
Alert, yet weary... like a bird
That all night long has beat about a light.

The Gentile lover, that she charms and shrews,
Is one more pebble in the pack
For Sadie's mother,
Who greets him with her narrowed eyes
That hold some welcome back.
"What's to be done?" she'll say,
"When Sadie wants she takes...
Better than Bennie with his Christian woman...
A man is not so like,
If they should fight,
To call her Jew..."

Yet when she lies in bed
And the soft babble of their talk comes to her
And the silences...
I know she never sleeps
Till the keen draught blowing up the empty hall
Edges through her transom
And she hears his foot on the first stairs.

Sarah and Anna live on the floor above.
Sarah is swarthy and ill-dressed.
Life for her has no ritual.
She would break an ideal like an egg for the winged thing at the core.
Her mind is hard and brilliant and cutting like an acetylene torch.

If any impurities drift there, they must be burnt up as in a clear flame.
It is droll that she should work in a pants factory.
--Yet where else... tousled and collar awry at her olive throat.
Besides her hands are unkempt.
With English... and everything... there is so little time.
She reads without bias--
Doubting clamorously--
Psychology, plays, science, philosophies--
Those giant flowers that have bloomed and withered, scattering their seed...
--And out of this young forcing soil what growth may come--
 what amazing blossomings.

Anna is different.
One is always aware of Anna, and the young men turn their heads
 to look at her.
She has the appeal of a folk-song
And her cheap clothes are always in rhythm.
When the strike was on she gave half her pay.
She would give anything--save the praise that is hers
And the love of her lyric body.

But Sarah's desire covets nothing apart.
She would share all things...
Even her lover.

III

The sturdy Ghetto children
March by the parade,
Waving their toy flags,
Prancing to the bugles--
Lusty, unafraid...
Shaking little fire sticks

At the night--
The old blinking night--
Swerving out of the way,
Wrapped in her darkness like a shawl.

But a small girl
Cowers apart.
Her braided head,
Shiny as a black-bird's
In the gleam of the torch-light,
Is poised as for flight.
Her eyes have the glow
Of darkened lights.

She stammers in Yiddish,
But I do not understand,
And there flits across her face
A shadow
As of a drawn blind.
I give her an orange,
Large and golden,
And she looks at it blankly.
I take her little cold hand and try to draw her to me,
But she is stiff...
Like a doll...

Suddenly she darts through the crowd
Like a little white panic
Blown along the night--
Away from the terror of oncoming feet...
And drums rattling like curses in red roaring mouths...
And torches spluttering silver fire
And lights that nose out hiding-places...

To the night--
Squatting like a hunchback
Under the curved stoop--
The old mammy-night
That has outlived beauty and knows the ways of fear--
The night--wide-opening crooked and comforting arms,
Hiding her as in a voluminous skirt.

The sturdy Ghetto children
March by the parade,
Waving their toy flags,
Prancing to the bugles,
Lusty, unafraid.
But I see a white frock
And eyes like hooded lights
Out of the shadow of pogroms
Watching... watching...

IV

Calicoes and furs,
Pocket-books and scarfs,
Razor strops and knives
(Patterns in check...)

Olive hands and russet head,
Pickles red and coppery,
Green pickles, brown pickles,
(Patterns in tapestry...)

Coral beads, blue beads,
Beads of pearl and amber,
Gewgaws, beauty pins--

Bijoutry for chits--
Darting rays of violet,
Amethyst and jade...
All the colors out to play,
Jumbled iridescently...
(Patterns in stained glass
Shivered into bits!)

Nooses of gay ribbon
Tugging at one's sleeve,
Dainty little garters
Hanging out their sign...
Here a pout of frilly things--
There a sonsy feather...
(White beards, black beards
Like knots in the weave...)

And ah, the little babies--
Shiny black-eyed babies--
(Half a million pink toes
Wriggling altogether.)
Baskets full of babies
Like grapes on a vine.

Mothers waddling in and out,
Making all things right--
Picking up the slipped threads
In Grand street at night--
Grand street like a great bazaar,
Crowded like a float,
Bulging like a crazy quilt
Stretched on a line.

But nearer seen
This litter of the East
Takes on a garbled majesty.

The herded stalls
In dissolute array...
The glitter and the jumbled finery
And strangely juxtaposed
Cans, paper, rags
And colors decomposing,
Faded like old hair,
With flashes of barbaric hues
And eyes of mystery...
Flung
Like an ancient tapestry of motley weave
Upon the open wall of this new land.

Here, a tawny-headed girl...
Lemons in a greenish broth
And a huge earthen bowl
By a bronzed merchant
With a tall black lamb's wool cap upon his head...
He has no glance for her.
His thrifty eyes
Bend--glittering, intent
Their hoarded looks
Upon his merchandise,
As though it were some splendid cloth
Or sumptuous raiment
Stitched in gold and red...

He seldom talks
Save of the goods he spreads--

The meager cotton with its dismal flower--
But with his skinny hands
That hover like two hawks
Above some luscious meat,
He fingers lovingly each calico,
As though it were a gorgeous shawl,
Or costly vesture
Wrought in silken thread,
Or strange bright carpet
Made for sandaled feet...

Here an old grey scholar stands.
His brooding eyes--
That hold long vistas without end
Of caravans and trees and roads,
And cities dwindling in remembrance--
Bend mostly on his tapes and thread.

What if they tweak his beard--
These raw young seed of Israel
Who have no backward vision in their eyes--
And mock him as he sways
Above the sunken arches of his feet--
They find no peg to hang their taunts upon.
His soul is like a rock
That bears a front worn smooth
By the coarse friction of the sea,
And, unperturbed, he keeps his bitter peace.

What if a rigid arm and stuffed blue shape,
Backed by a nickel star
Does prod him on,
Taking his proud patience for humility...

All gutters are as one
To that old race that has been thrust
From off the curbstones of the world...
And he smiles with the pale irony
Of one who holds
The wisdom of the Talmud stored away
In his mind's lavender.

But this young trader,
Born to trade as to a caul,
Peddles the notions of the hour.
The gestures of the craft are his
And all the lore
As when to hold, withdraw, persuade, advance...
And be it gum or flags,
Or clean-all or the newest thing in tags,
Demand goes to him as the bee to flower.
And he--appraising
All who come and go
With his amazing
Slight-of-mind and glance
And nimble thought
And nature balanced like the scales at nought--
Looks Westward where the trade-lights glow,
And sees his vision rise--
A tape-ruled vision,
Circumscribed in stone--
Some fifty stories to the skies.

V

As I sit in my little fifth-floor room--
Bare,
Save for bed and chair,
And coppery stains
Left by seeping rains
On the low ceiling
And green plaster walls,
Where when night falls
Golden lady-bugs
Come out of their holes,
And roaches, sepia-brown, consort...
I hear bells pealing
Out of the gray church at Rutgers street,
Holding its high-flung cross above the Ghetto,
And, one floor down across the court,
The parrot screaming:
Vorwaerts... Vorwaerts...

The parrot frowsy-white,
Everlastingly swinging
On its iron bar.

A little old woman,
With a wig of smooth black hair
Gummed about her shrunken brows,
Comes sometimes on the fire escape.
An old stooped mother,
The left shoulder low
With that uneven droopiness that women know
Who have suckled many young...

Yet I have seen no other than the parrot there.

I watch her mornings as she shakes her rugs
Feebly, with futile reach
And fingers without clutch.
Her thews are slack
And curved the ruined back
And flesh empurpled like old meat,
Yet each conspires
To feed those guttering fires
With which her eyes are quick.

On Friday nights
Her candles signal
Infinite fine rays
To other windows,
Coupling other lights,
Linking the tenements
Like an endless prayer.

She seems less lonely than the bird
That day by day about the dismal house
Screams out his frenzied word...
That night by night--
If a dog yelps
Or a cat yawls
Or a sick child whines,
Or a door screaks on its hinges,
Or a man and woman fight--
Sends his cry above the huddled roofs:
Vorwaerts... Vorwaerts...

VI

In this dingy cafe
The old men sit muffled in woollens.
Everything is faded, shabby, colorless, old...
The chairs, loose-jointed,
Creaking like old bones--
The tables, the waiters, the walls,
Whose mottled plaster
Blends in one tone with the old flesh.

Young life and young thought are alike barred,
And no unheralded noises jolt old nerves,
And old wheezy breaths
Pass around old thoughts, dry as snuff,
And there is no divergence and no friction
Because life is flattened and ground as by many mills.

And it is here the Committee--
Sweet-breathed and smooth of skin
And supple of spine and knee,
With shining unpouched eyes
And the blood, high-powered,
Leaping in flexible arteries--
The insolent, young, enthusiastic, undiscriminating Committee,
Who would placard tombstones
And scatter leaflets even in graves,
Comes trampling with sacrilegious feet!

The old men turn stiffly,
Mumbling to each other.
They are gentle and torpid and busy with eating.

But one lifts a face of clayish pallor,
There is a dull fury in his eyes, like little rusty grates.
He rises slowly,
Trembling in his many swathings like an awakened mummy,
Ridiculous yet terrible.
--And the Committee flings him a waste glance,
Dropping a leaflet by his plate.

A lone fire flickers in the dusty eyes.
The lips chant inaudibly.
The warped shrunken body straightens like a tree.
And he curses...
With uplifted arms and perished fingers,
Claw-like, clutching...
So centuries ago
The old men cursed Acosta,
When they, prophetic, heard upon their sepulchres
Those feet that may not halt nor turn aside for ancient things.

VII

Here in this room, bare like a barn,
Egos gesture one to the other--
Naked, unformed, unwinged
Egos out of the shell,
Examining, searching, devouring--
Avid alike for the flower or the dung...
(Having no dainty antennae for the touch and withdrawal--
Only the open maw...)

Egos cawing,
Expanding in the mean egg...
Little squat tailors with unkempt faces,

Pale as lard,
Fur-makers, factory-hands, shop-workers,
News-boys with battling eyes
And bodies yet vibrant with the momentum of long runs,
Here and there a woman...

Words, words, words,
Pattering like hail,
Like hail falling without aim...
Egos rampant,
Screaming each other down.
One motions perpetually,
Waving arms like overgrowths.
He has burning eyes and a cough
And a thin voice piping
Like a flute among trombones.

One, red-bearded, rearing
A welter of maimed face bashed in from some old wound,
Garbles Max Stirner.
His words knock each other like little wooden blocks.
No one heeds him,
And a lank boy with hair over his eyes
Pounds upon the table.
--He is chairman.

Egos yet in the primer,
Hearing world-voices
Chanting grand arias...
Majors resonant,
Stunning with sound...
Baffling minors
Half-heard like rain on pools...

Majestic discordances
Greater than harmonies...
--Gleaning out of it all
Passion, bewilderment, pain...

Egos yearning with the world-old want in their eyes--
Hurt hot eyes that do not sleep enough...
Striving with infinite effort,
Frustrate yet ever pursuing
The great white Liberty,
Trailing her dissolving glory over each hard-won barricade--
Only to fade anew...

Egos crying out of unkempt deeps
And waving their dreams like flags--
Multi-colored dreams,
Winged and glorious...

A gas jet throws a stunted flame,
Vaguely illumining the groping faces.
And through the uncurtained window
Falls the waste light of stars,
As cold as wise men's eyes...
Indifferent great stars,
Fortuitously glancing
At the secret meeting in this shut-in room,
Bare as a manger.

VIII

Lights go out
And the stark trunks of the factories
Melt into the drawn darkness,
Sheathing like a seamless garment.

And mothers take home their babies,
Waxen and delicately curled,
Like little potted flowers closed under the stars.

Lights go out
And the young men shut their eyes,
But life turns in them...

Life in the cramped ova
Tearing and rending asunder its living cells...
Wars, arts, discoveries, rebellions, travails, immolations,
 cataclysms, hates...
Pent in the shut flesh.
And the young men twist on their beds in languor and dizziness
 unsupportable...
Their eyes--heavy and dimmed
With dust of long oblivions in the gray pulp behind--
Staring as through a choked glass.
And they gaze at the moon--throwing off a faint heat--
The moon, blond and burning, creeping to their cots
Softly, as on naked feet...
Lolling on the coverlet... like a woman offering her white body.

Nude glory of the moon!
That leaps like an athlete on the bosoms of the young girls stripped

of their linens;
Stroking their breasts that are smooth and cool as mother-of-pearl
Till the nipples tingle and burn as though little lips plucked at them.
They shudder and grow faint.
And their ears are filled as with a delirious rhapsody,
That Life, like a drunken player,
Strikes out of their clear white bodies
As out of ivory keys.

Lights go out...
And the great lovers linger in little groups, still passionately debating,
Or one may walk in silence, listening only to the still summons of Life--
Life making the great Demand...
Calling its new Christs...
Till tears come, blurring the stars
That grow tender and comforting like the eyes of comrades;
And the moon rolls behind the Battery
Like a word molten out of the mouth of God.

Lights go out...
And colors rush together,
Fusing and floating away...
Pale worn gold like the settings of old jewels...
Mauves, exquisite, tremulous, and luminous purples
And burning spires in aureoles of light
Like shimmering auras.

They are covering up the pushcarts...
Now all have gone save an old man with mirrors--
Little oval mirrors like tiny pools.
He shuffles up a darkened street
And the moon burnishes his mirrors till they shine like phosphorus...
The moon like a skull,

Staring out of eyeless sockets at the old men trundling home the pushcarts.

IX

A sallow dawn is in the sky
As I enter my little green room.
Sadie's light is still burning...
Without, the frail moon
Worn to a silvery tissue,
Throws a faint glamour on the roofs,
And down the shadowy spires
Lights tip-toe out...
Softly as when lovers close street doors.

Out of the Battery
A little wind
Stirs idly--as an arm
Trails over a boat's side in dalliance--
Rippling the smooth dead surface of the heat,
And Hester street,
Like a forlorn woman over-born
By many babies at her teats,
Turns on her trampled bed to meet the day.

LIFE!
Startling, vigorous life,
That squirms under my touch,
And baffles me when I try to examine it,
Or hurls me back without apology.
Leaving my ego ruffled and preening itself.

Life,
Articulate, shrill,

Screaming in provocative assertion,
Or out of the black and clotted gutters,
Piping in silvery thin
Sweet staccato
Of children's laughter,

Or clinging over the pushcarts
Like a litter of tiny bells
Or the jingle of silver coins,
Perpetually changing hands,
Or like the Jordan somberly
Swirling in tumultuous uncharted tides,
Surface-calm.

Electric currents of life,
Throwing off thoughts like sparks,
Glittering, disappearing,
Making unknown circuits,
Or out of spent particles stirring
Feeble contortions in old faiths
Passing before the new.

Long nights argued away
In meeting halls
Back of interminable stairways--
In Roumanian wine-shops
And little Russian tea-rooms...

Feet echoing through deserted streets
In the soft darkness before dawn...
Brows aching, throbbing, burning--
Life leaping in the shaken flesh
Like flame at an asbestos curtain.

Life--
Pent, overflowing
Stoops and facades,
Jostling, pushing, contriving,
Seething as in a great vat...

Bartering, changing, extorting,
Dreaming, debating, aspiring,
Astounding, indestructible
Life of the Ghetto...

Strong flux of life,
Like a bitter wine
Out of the bloody stills of the world...
Out of the Passion eternal.

MANHATTAN LIGHTS

MANHATTAN

Out of the night you burn, Manhattan,
In a vesture of gold--
Span of innumerable arcs,
Flaring and multiplying--
Gold at the uttermost circles fading
Into the tenderest hint of jade,
Or fusing in tremulous twilight blues,
Robing the far-flung offices,
Scintillant-storied, forking flame,
Or soaring to luminous amethyst
Over the steeples aureoled--

Diaphanous gold,
Veiling the Woolworth, argently
Rising slender and stark
Mellifluous-shrill as a vender's cry,
And towers squatting graven and cold
On the velvet bales of the dark,
And the Singer's appraising
Indolent idol's eye,
And night like a purple cloth unrolled--

Nebulous gold
Throwing an ephemeral glory about life's vanishing points,
Wherein you burn...
You of unknown voltage
Whirling on your axis...
Scrawling vermillion signatures
Over the night's velvet hoarding...
Insolent, towering spherical
To apices ever shifting.

BROADWAY

Light!
Innumerable ions of light,
Kindling, irradiating,
All to their foci tending...

Light that jingles like anklet chains
On bevies of little lithe twinkling feet,
Or clingles in myriad vibrations
Like trillions of porcelain
Vases shattering...

Light over the laminae of roofs,
Diffusing in shimmering nebulae
About the night's boundaries,
Or billowing in pearly foam
Submerging the low-lying stars...

Light for the feast prolonged--
Captive light in the goblets quivering...
Sparks evanescent

Struck of meeting looks--
Fringed eyelids leashing
Sheathed and leaping lights...
Infinite bubbles of light
Bursting, reforming...
Silvery filings of light
Incessantly falling...
Scintillant, sided dust of light
Out of the white flares of Broadway--
Like a great spurious diamond
In the night's corsage faceted...

Broadway,
In ambuscades of light,
Drawing the charmed multitudes
With the slow suction of her breath--
Dangling her naked soul
Behind the blinding gold of eunuch lights
That wind about her like a bodyguard.

Or like a huge serpent, iridescent-scaled,
Trailing her coruscating length
Over the night prostrate--
Triumphant poised,
Her hydra heads above the avenues,
Values appraising
And her avid eyes
Glistening with eternal watchfulness...

Broadway--
Out of her towers rampant,
Like an unsubtle courtezan
Reserving nought for some adventurous night.

FLOTSAM

Crass rays streaming from the vestibules;
Cafes glittering like jeweled teeth;
High-flung signs
Blinking yellow phosphorescent eyes;
Girls in black
Circling monotonously
About the orange lights...

Nothing to guess at...
Save the darkness above
Crouching like a great cat.

In the dim-lit square,
Where dishevelled trees
Tustle with the wind--the wind like a scythe
Mowing their last leaves--
Arcs shimmering through a greenish haze--
Pale oval arcs
Like ailing virgins,
Each out of a halo circumscribed,
Pallidly staring...

Figures drift upon the benches
With no more rustle than a dropped leaf settling--
Slovenly figures like untied parcels,
And papers wrapped about their knees
Huddled one to the other,
Cringing to the wind--
The sided wind,
Leaving no breach untried...

So many and all so still...
The fountain slobbering its stone basin
Is louder than They--
Flotsam of the five oceans
Here on this raft of the world.

This old man's head
Has found a woman's shoulder.
The wind juggles with her shawl
That flaps about them like a sail,
And splashes her red faded hair
Over the salt stubble of his chin.
A light foam is on his lips,
As though dreams surged in him
Breaking and ebbing away...
And the bare boughs shuffle above him
And the twigs rattle like dice...

She--diffused like a broken beetle--
Sprawls without grace,
Her face gray as asphalt,
Her jaws sagging as on loosened hinges...
Shadows ply about her mouth--
Nimble shadows out of the jigging tree,
That dances above her its dance of dry bones.

II

A uniformed front,
Paunched;
A glance like a blow,
The swing of an arm,

Verved, vigorous;
Boot-heels clanking
In metallic rhythm;
The blows of a baton,
Quick, staccato...

--There is a rustling along the benches
As of dried leaves raked over...
And the old man lifts a shaking palsied hand,
Tucking the displaced paper about his knees.

Colder...
And a frost under foot,
Acid, corroding,
Eating through worn bootsoles.

Drab forms blur into greenish vapor.
Through boughs like cross-bones,
Pale arcs flare and shiver
Like lilies in a wind.

High over Broadway
A far-flung sign
Glitters in indigo darkness
And spurts again rhythmically,
Spraying great drops
Red as a hemorrhage.

SPRING

A spring wind on the Bowery,
Blowing the fluff of night shelters
Off bedraggled garments,
And agitating the gutters, that eject little spirals of vapor
Like lewd growths.

Bare-legged children stamp in the puddles, splashing each other,
One--with a choir-boy's face
Twits me as I pass...
The word, like a muddied drop,
Seems to roll over and not out of
The bowed lips,
Yet dewy red
And sweetly immature.

People sniff the air with an upward look--
Even the mite of a girl
Who never plays...
Her mother smiles at her
With eyes like vacant lots
Rimming vistas of mean streets
And endless washing days...
Yet with sun on the lines
And a drying breeze.

The old candy woman
Shivers in the young wind.
Her eyes--littered with memories
Like ancient garrets,
Or dusty unaired rooms where someone died--

Ask nothing of the spring.

But a pale pink dream
Trembles about this young girl's body,
Draping it like a glowing aura.

She gloats in a mirror
Over her gaudy hat,
With its flower God never thought of...

And the dream, unrestrained,
Floats about the loins of a soldier,
Where it quivers a moment,
Warming to a crimson
Like the scarf of a toreador...

But the delicate gossamer breaks at his contact
And recoils to her in strands of shattered rose.

BOWERY AFTERNOON

Drab discoloration
Of faces, facades, pawn-shops,
Second-hand clothing,
Smoky and fly-blown glass of lunch-rooms,
Odors of rancid life...

Deadly uniformity
Of eyes and windows
Alike devoid of light...
Holes wherein life scratches--

Mangy life
Nosing to the gutter's end...

Show-rooms and mimic pillars
Flaunting out of their gaudy vestibules
Bosoms and posturing thighs...

Over all the Elevated
Droning like a bloated fly.

PROMENADE

Undulant rustlings,
Of oncoming silk,
Rhythmic, incessant,
Like the motion of leaves...
Fragments of color
In glowing surprises...
Pink inuendoes
Hooded in gray
Like buds in a cobweb
Pearled at dawn...
Glimpses of green
And blurs of gold
And delicate mauves
That snatch at youth...
And bodies all rosily
Fleshed for the airing,
In warm velvety surges
Passing imperious, slow...

Women drift into the limousines
That shut like silken caskets
On gems half weary of their glittering...
Lamps open like pale moon flowers...
Arcs are radiant opals
Strewn along the dusk...
No common lights invade.
And spires rise like litanies--
Magnificats of stone
Over the white silence of the arcs,
Burning in perpetual adoration.

THE FOG

Out of the lamp-bestarred and clouded dusk--
Snaring, illuding, concealing,
Magically conjuring--
Turning to fairy-coaches
Beetle-backed limousines
Scampering under the great Arch--
Making a decoy of blue overalls
And mystery of a scarlet shawl--
Indolently--
Knowing no impediment of its sure advance--
Descends the fog.

FACES

A late snow beats
With cold white fists upon the tenements--
Hurriedly drawing blinds and shutters,
Like tall old slatterns
Pulling aprons about their heads.

Lights slanting out of Mott Street
Gibber out,
Or dribble through bar-room slits,
Anonymous shapes
Conniving behind shuttered panes
Caper and disappear...
Where the Bowery
Is throbbing like a fistula
Back of her ice-scabbed fronts.

Livid faces
Glimmer in furtive doorways,
Or spill out of the black pockets of alleys,
Smears of faces like muddied beads,
Making a ghastly rosary
The night mumbles over
And the snow with its devilish and silken whisper...
Patrolling arcs
Blowing shrill blasts over the Bread Line
Stalk them as they pass,
Silent as though accouched of the darkness,
And the wind noses among them,
 Like a skunk
That roots about the heart...

Colder:
And the Elevated slams upon the silence
Like a ponderous door.
Then all is still again,
Save for the wind fumbling over
The emptily swaying faces--
The wind rummaging
Like an old Jew...

Faces in glimmering rows...
(No sign of the abject life--
Not even a blasphemy...)
But the spindle legs keep time
To a limping rhythm,
And the shadows twitch upon the snow
 Convulsively--
As though death played
With some ungainly dolls.

LABOR

DEBRIS

I love those spirits
That men stand off and point at,
Or shudder and hood up their souls--
Those ruined ones,
Where Liberty has lodged an hour
And passed like flame,
Bursting asunder the too small house.

DEDICATION

I would be a torch unto your hand,
A lamp upon your forehead, Labor,
In the wild darkness before the Dawn
That I shall never see...

We shall advance together, my Beloved,
Awaiting the mighty ushering...
Together we shall make the last grand charge

And ride with gorgeous Death
With all her spangles on
And cymbals clashing...
And you shall rush on exultant as I fall--
Scattering a brief fire about your feet...

Let it be so...
Better--while life is quick
And every pain immense and joy supreme,
And all I have and am
Flames upward to the dream...
Than like a taper forgotten in the dawn,
Burning out the wick.

THE SONG OF IRON

I

Not yet hast Thou sounded
Thy clangorous music,
Whose strings are under the mountains...
Not yet hast Thou spoken
The blooded, implacable Word...

But I hear in the Iron singing--
In the triumphant roaring of the steam and pistons pounding--
Thy barbaric exhortation...
And the blood leaps in my arteries, unreproved,
Answering Thy call...
All my spirit is inundated with the tumultuous passion of Thy Voice,
And sings exultant with the Iron,

For now I know I too am of Thy Chosen...

Oh fashioned in fire--
Needing flame for Thy ultimate word--
Behold me, a cupola
Poured to Thy use!

Heed not my tremulous body
That faints in the grip of Thy gauntlet.
Break it... and cast it aside...
But make of my spirit
That dares and endures
Thy crucible...
Pour through my soul
Thy molten, world-whelming song.

... Here at Thy uttermost gate
Like a new Mary, I wait...

II

Charge the blast furnace, workman...
Open the valves--
Drive the fires high...
(Night is above the gates).

How golden-hot the ore is
From the cupola spurting,
Tossing the flaming petals
Over the silt and furnace ash--
Blown leaves, devastating,
Falling about the world...

Out of the furnace mouth--
Out of the giant mouth--
The raging, turgid, mouth--
Fall fiery blossoms
Gold with the gold of buttercups
In a field at sunset,
Or huskier gold of dandelions,
Warmed in sun-leavings,
Or changing to the paler hue
At the creamy hearts of primroses.

Charge the converter, workman--
Tired from the long night?
But the earth shall suck up darkness--
The earth that holds so much...
And out of these molten flowers,
Shall shape the heavy fruit...

Then open the valves--
Drive the fires high,
Your blossoms nurturing.
(Day is at the gates
And a young wind...)

Put by your rod, comrade,
And look with me, shading your eyes...
Do you not see--
Through the lucent haze
Out of the converter rising--
In the spirals of fire
Smiting and blinding,
A shadowy shape
White as a flame of sacrifice,

Like a lily swaying?

III

The ore leaping in the crucibles,
The ore communicant,
Sending faint thrills along the leads...
Fire is running along the roots of the mountains...
I feel the long recoil of earth
As under a mighty quickening...
(Dawn is aglow in the light of the Iron...)
All palpitant, I wait...

IV

Here ye, Dictators--late Lords of the Iron,
Shut in your council rooms, palsied, depowered--
The blooded, implacable Word?
Not whispered in cloture, one to the other,
(Brother in fear of the fear of his brother...)
But chanted and thundered
On the brazen, articulate tongues of the Iron
Babbling in flame...

Sung to the rhythm of prisons dismantled,
Manacles riven and ramparts defaced...
(Hearts death-anointed yet hearing life calling...)
Ankle chains bursting and gallows unbraced...

Sung to the rhythm of arsenals burning...
Clangor of iron smashing on iron,
Turmoil of metal and dissonant baying

Of mail-sided monsters shattered asunder...

Hulks of black turbines all mangled and roaring,
Battering egress through ramparted walls...
Mouthing of engines, made rabid with power,
Into the holocaust snorting and plunging...

Mighty converters torn from their axis,
Flung to the furnaces, vomiting fire,
Jumbled in white-heaten masses disshapen...
Writhing in flame-tortured levers of iron...

Gnashing of steel serpents twisting and dying...
Screeching of steam-glutted cauldrons rending...
Shock of leviathans prone on each other...
Scaled flanks touching, ore entering ore...
Steel haunches closing and grappling and swaying
In the waltz of the mating locked mammoths of iron,
Tasting the turbulent fury of living,
Mad with a moment's exuberant living!
Crash of devastating hammers despoiling..
Hands inexorable, marring
What hands had so cunningly moulded...

Structures of steel welded, subtily tempered,
Marvelous wrought of the wizards of ore,
Torn into octaves discordantly clashing,
Chords never final but onward progressing
In monstrous fusion of sound ever smiting on sound
 in mad vortices whirling...

Till the ear, tortured, shrieks for cessation
Of the raving inharmonies hatefully mingling...

The fierce obligato the steel pipes are screaming...
The blare of the rude molten music of Iron...

FRANK LITTLE AT CALVARY

I

He walked under the shadow of the Hill
Where men are fed into the fires
And walled apart...
Unarmed and alone,
He summoned his mates from the pit's mouth
Where tools rested on the floors
And great cranes swung
Unemptied, on the iron girders.
And they, who were the Lords of the Hill,
Were seized with a great fear,
When they heard out of the silence of wheels
The answer ringing
In endless reverberations
Under the mountain...

So they covered up their faces
And crept upon him as he slept...
Out of eye-holes in black cloth
They looked upon him who had flung
Between them and their ancient prey
The frail barricade of his life...
And when night--that has connived at so much--
Was heavy with the unborn day,
They haled him from his bed...

Who might know of that wild ride?
Only the bleak Hill--
The red Hill, vigilant,
Like a blood-shot eye
In the black mask of night--
Dared watch them as they raced
By each blind-folded street
Godiva might have ridden down...
But when they stopped beside the Place,
I know he turned his face
Wistfully to the accessory night...

And when he saw--against the sky,
Sagged like a silken net
Under its load of stars--
The black bridge poised
Like a gigantic spider motionless...
I know there was a silence in his heart,
As of a frozen sea,
Where some half lifted arm, mid-way
Wavers, and drops heavily...

I know he waved to life,
And that life signaled back, transcending space,
To each high-powered sense,
So that he missed no gesture of the wind
Drawing the shut leaves close...
So that he saw the light on comrades' faces
Of camp fires out of sight...
And the savor of meat and bread
Blew in his nostrils... and the breath
Of unrailed spaces
Where shut wild clover smelled as sweet

As a virgin in her bed.

I know he looked once at America,
Quiescent, with her great flanks on the globe,
And once at the skies whirling above him...
Then all that he had spoken against
And struck against and thrust against
Over the frail barricade of his life
Rushed between him and the stars...

II

Life thunders on...
Over the black bridge
The line of lighted cars
Creeps like a monstrous serpent
Spooring gold...

Watchman, what of the track?

Night... silence... stars...
All's Well!

III

Light...
(Breaking mists...
Hills gliding like hands out of a slipping hold...)
Light over the pit mouths,
Streaming in tenuous rays down the black gullets of the Hill...
(The copper, insensate, sleeping in the buried lode.)
Light...
Forcing the clogged windows of arsenals...

Probing with long sentient fingers in the copper chips...
Gleaming metallic and cold
In numberless slivers of steel...
Light over the trestles and the iron clips
Of the black bridge--poised like a gigantic spider motionless--
Sweet inquisition of light, like a child's wonder...
Intrusive, innocently staring light
That nothing appals...

Light in the slow fumbling summer leaves,
Cooing and calling
All winged and avid things
Waking the early flies, keen to the scent...
Green-jeweled iridescent flies
Unerringly steering--
Swarming over the blackened lips,
The young day sprays with indiscriminate gold...

Watchman, what of the Hill?

Wheels turn;
The laden cars
Go rumbling to the mill,
And Labor walks beside the mules...
All's Well with the Hill!

SPIRES

Spires of Grace Church,
For you the workers of the world
Travailed with the mountains...
Aborting their own dreams
Till the dream of you arose--
Beautiful, swaddled in stone--
Scorning their hands.

THE LEGION OF IRON

They pass through the great iron gates--
Men with eyes gravely discerning,
Skilled to appraise the tunnage of cranes
Or split an inch into thousandths--
Men tempered by fire as the ore is
And planned to resistance
Like steel that has cooled in the trough;
Silent of purpose, inflexible, set to fulfilment--
To conquer, withstand, overthrow...
Men mannered to large undertakings,
Knowing force as a brother
And power as something to play with,
Seeing blood as a slip of the iron,
To be wiped from the tools
Lest they rust.

But what if they stood aside,
Who hold the earth so careless in the crook of their arms?

What of the flamboyant cities
And the lights guttering out like candles in a wind...
And the armies halted...
And the train mid-way on the mountain
And idle men chaffing across the trenches...
And the cursing and lamentation
And the clamor for grain shut in the mills of the world?
What if they stayed apart,
Inscrutably smiling,
Leaving the ground encumbered with dead wire
And the sea to row-boats
And the lands marooned--
Till Time should like a paralytic sit,
A mildewed hulk above the nations squatting?

FUEL

What of the silence of the keys
And silvery hands? The iron sings...
Though bows lie broken on the strings,
The fly-wheels turn eternally...

Bring fuel--drive the fires high...
Throw all this artist-lumber in
And foolish dreams of making things...
(Ten million men are called to die.)

As for the common men apart,
Who sweat to keep their common breath,
And have no hour for books or art--
What dreams have these to hide from death!

A TOAST

Not your martyrs anointed of heaven--
 The ages are red where they trod--
But the Hunted--the world's bitter leaven--
 Who smote at your imbecile God--

A being to pander and fawn to,
 To propitiate, flatter and dread
As a thing that your souls are in pawn to,
 A Dealer who traffics the dead;

A Trader with greed never sated,
 Who barters the souls in his snares,
That were trapped in the lusts he created,
 For incense and masses and prayers--

They are crushed in the coils of your halters;
 'Twere well--by the creeds ye have nursed--
That ye send up a cry from your altars,
 A mass for the Martyrs Accursed;

A passionate prayer from reprieval
 For the Brotherhood not understood--
For the Heroes who died for the evil,
 Believing the evil was good.

To the Breakers, the Bold, the Despoilers,
 Who dreamed of a world over-thrown...
They who died for the millions of toilers--
 Few--fronting the nations alone!

--To the Outlawed of men and the Branded,
 Whether hated or hating they fell--
I pledge the devoted, red-handed,
 Unfaltering Heroes of Hell!

ACCIDENTALS

"THE EVERLASTING RETURN"

It is dark... so dark, I remember the sun on Chios...
It is still... so still, I hear the beat of our paddles on the Aegean...

Ten times we had watched the moon
Rise like a thin white virgin out of the waters
And round into a full maternity...
For thrice ten moons we had touched no flesh
Save the man flesh on either hand
That was black and bitter and salt and scaled by the sea.

The Athenian boy sat on my left...
His hair was yellow as corn steeped in wine...
And on my right was Phildar the Carthaginian,
Grinning Phildar
With his mouth pulled taut as by reins from his black gapped teeth.
Many a whip had coiled about him
And his shoulders were rutted deep as wet ground under chariot wheels,
And his skin was red and tough as a bull's hide cured in the sun.
He did not sing like the other slaves,
But when a big wind came up he screamed with it.
And always he looked out to sea,
Save when he tore at his fish ends

Or spat across me at the Greek boy, whose mouth was red and apart
 like an opened fruit.

We had rowed from dawn and the green galley hard at our stern.
She was green and squat and skulked close to the sea.
All day the tish of their paddles had tickled our ears,
And when night came on
And little naked stars dabbled in the water
And half the crouching moon
Slid over the silver belly of the sea thick-scaled with light,
We heard them singing at their oars...
We who had no breath for song.

There was no sound in our boat
Save the clingle of wrist chains
And the sobbing of the young Greek.
I cursed him that his hair blew in my mouth, tasting salt of the sea...
I cursed him that his oar kept ill time...
When he looked at me I cursed him again,
That his eyes were soft as a woman's.

How long... since their last shell gouged our batteries?
How long... since we rose at aim with a sleuth moon astern?
(It was the damned green moon that nosed us out...
The moon that flushed our periscope till it shone like a silver flame...)

They loosed each man's right hand
As the galley spent on our decks...
And amazed and bloodied we reared half up
And fought askew with the left hand shackled...
But a zigzag fire leapt in our sockets
And knotted our thews like string...
Our thews grown stiff as a crooked spine that would not straighten...

How long... since our gauges fell
And the sea shoved us under?
It is dark... so dark...
Darkness presses hairy-hot
Where three make crowded company...
And the rank steel smells....
It is still... so still...
I seem to hear the wind
On the dimpled face of the water fathoms above...

It was still... so still... we three that were left alive
Stared in each other's faces...
But three make bitter company at one man's bread...
And our hate grew sharp and bright as the moon's edge in the water.

One grinned with his mouth awry from the long gapped teeth...
And one shivered and whined like a gull as the waves pawed us over...
But one struck with his hate in his hand...

After that I remember
Only the dead men's oars that flapped in the sea...
The dead men's oars that rattled and clicked like idiots' tongues.

It is still... so still, with the jargon of engines quiet.
We three awaiting the crunch of the sea
Reach our hands in the dark and touch each other's faces...
We three sheathing hate in our hearts...
But when hate shall have made its circuit,
Our bones will be loving company
Here in the sea's den...
And one whimpers and cries on his God
And one sits sullenly

But both draw away from me...
For I am the pyre their memories burn on...
Like black flames leaping
Our fiery gestures light the walled-in darkness of the sea...
The sea that kneels above us...
And makes no sign.

PALESTINE

Old plant of Asia--
Mutilated vine
Holding earth's leaping sap
In every stem and shoot
That lopped off, sprouts again--
Why should you seek a plateau walled about,
Whose garden is the world?

THE SONG

That day, in the slipping of torsos and straining flanks
 on the bloodied ooze of fields plowed by the iron,
And the smoke bluish near earth and bronze in the sunshine
 floating like cotton-down,
And the harsh and terrible screaming,
And that strange vibration at the roots of us...
Desire, fierce, like a song...
And we heard
(Do you remember?)

All the Red Cross bands on Fifth avenue
And bugles in little home towns
And children's harmonicas bleating

 America!

And after...
(Do you remember?)
The drollery of the wind on our faces,
And horizons reeling,
And the terror of the plain
Heaving like a gaunt pelvis to the sun...
Under us--threshing and twanging
Torn-up roots of the Song...

TO THE OTHERS

I see you, refulgent ones,
Burning so steadily
Like big white arc lights...
There are so many of you.
I like to watch you weaving--
Altogether and with precision
Each his ray--
Your tracery of light,
Making a shining way about America.

I note your infinite reactions--
In glassware
And sequin
And puddles
And bits of jet--
And here and there a diamond...

But you do not yet see me,
Who am a torch blown along the wind,
Flickering to a spark
But never out.

BABEL

Oh, God did cunningly, there at Babel--
Not mere tongues dividing, but soul from soul,
So that never again should men be able
To fashion one infinite, towering whole.

THE FIDDLER

In a little Hungarian cafe
Men and women are drinking
Yellow wine in tall goblets.

Through the milky haze of the smoke,
The fiddler, under-sized, blond,
Leans to his violin
As to the breast of a woman.
Red hair kindles to fire
On the black of his coat-sleeve,
Where his white thin hand
Trembles and dives,
Like a sliver of moonlight,
When wind has broken the water.

DAWN WIND

Wind, just arisen--
(Off what cool mattress of marsh-moss
In tented boughs leaf-drawn before the stars,
Or niche of cliff under the eagles?)
You of living things,
So gay and tender and full of play--
Why do you blow on my thoughts--like cut flowers
Gathered and laid to dry on this paper, rolled out of dead wood?

I see you
Shaking that flower at me with soft invitation
And frisking away,
Deliciously rumpling the grass...

So you fluttered the curtains about my cradle,
Prattling of fields
Before I had had my milk...
Did I stir on my pillow, making to follow you, Fleet One?
I--swaddled, unwinged, like a bird in the egg.

Let be
My dreams that crackle under your breath...
You have the dust of the world to blow on...
Do not tag me and dance away, looking back...
I am too old to play with you,
Eternal Child.

NORTH WIND

I love you, malcontent
Male wind--
Shaking the pollen from a flower
Or hurling the sea backward from the grinning sand.

Blow on and over my dreams...
Scatter my sick dreams...
Throw your lusty arms about me...
Envelop all my hot body...
Carry me to pine forests--
Great, rough-bearded forests...
Bring me to stark plains and steppes...
I would have the North to-night--
The cold, enduring North.

And if we should meet the Snow,
Whirling in spirals,
And he should blind my eyes...
Ally, you will defend me--
You will hold me close,
Blowing on my eyelids.

THE DESTROYER

I am of the wind...
A wisp of the battering wind...

I trail my fingers along the Alps
And an avalanche falls in my wake...
I feel in my quivering length
When it buries the hamlet beneath...

I hurriedly sweep aside
The cities that clutter our path...
As we whirl about the circle of the globe...
As we tear at the pillars of the world...
Open to the wind,
The Destroyer!
The wind that is battering at your gates.

LULLABY

Rock-a-by baby, woolly and brown...
(There's a shout at the door an' a big red light...)
Lil' coon baby, mammy is down...
Han's that hold yuh are steady an' white...

Look piccaninny--such a gran' blaze
Lickin' up the roof an' the sticks of home--
Ever see the like in all yo' days!
--Cain't yuh sleep, mah bit-of-honey-comb?

Rock-a-by baby, up to the sky!
Look at the cherries driftin' by--
Bright red cherries spilled on the groun'--
Piping-hot cherries at nuthin' a poun'!

Hush, mah lil' black-bug--doan yuh weep.
Daddy's run away an' mammy's in a heap
By her own fron' door in the blazin' heat
Outah the shacks like warts on the street...

An' the singin' flame an' the gleeful crowd
Circlin' aroun'... won't mammy be proud!
With a stone at her hade an' a stone on her heart,
An' her mouth like a red plum, broken apart...

See where the blue an' khaki prance,
Adding brave colors to the dance
About the big bonfire white folks make--
Such gran' doin's fo' a lil' coon's sake!

Hear all the eagah feet runnin' in town--
See all the willin' han's reach outah night--
Han's that are wonderful, steady an' white!
To toss up a lil' babe, blinkin' an' brown...

Rock-a-by baby--higher an' higher!
Mammy is sleepin' an' daddy's run lame...
(Soun' may yuh sleep in yo' cradle o' fire!)
Rock-a-by baby, hushed in the flame...

(An incident of the East St. Louis Race Riots, when some white women
flung a living colored baby into the heart of a blazing fire.)

THE FOUNDLING

Snow wraiths circle us
Like washers of the dead,
Flapping their white wet cloths
Impatiently
About the grizzled head,
Where the coarse hair mats like grass,
And the efficient wind
With cold professional baste
Probes like a lancet
Through the cotton shirt...

About us are white cliffs and space.
No facades show,
Nor roof nor any spire...
All sheathed in snow...
The parasitic snow
That clings about them like a blight.

Only detached lights
Float hazily like greenish moons,
And endlessly
Down the whore-street,
Accouched and comforted and sleeping warm,
The blizzard waltzes with the night.

THE WOMAN WITH JEWELS

The woman with jewels sits in the cafe,
Spraying light like a fountain.
Diamonds glitter on her bulbous fingers
And on her arms, great as thighs,
Diamonds gush from her ear-lobes over the goitrous throat.
She is obesely beautiful.
Her eyes are full of bleared lights,
Like little pools of tar, spilled by a sailor in mad haste for shore...
And her mouth is scarlet and full--only a little crumpled--
 like a flower that has been pressed apart...

Why does she come alone to this obscure basement--
She who should have a litter and hand-maidens to support her
 on either side?

She ascends the stairway, and the waiters turn to look at her,
 spilling the soup.
The black satin dress is a little lifted, showing the dropsical legs
 in their silken fleshings...
The mountainous breasts tremble...
There is an agitation in her gems,
That quiver incessantly, emitting trillions of fiery rays...
She erupts explosive breaths...
Every step is an adventure
From this...
The serpent's tooth
Saved Cleopatra.

SUBMERGED

I have known only my own shallows--
Safe, plumbed places,
Where I was wont to preen myself.

But for the abyss
I wanted a plank beneath
And horizons...

I was afraid of the silence
And the slipping toe-hold...

Oh, could I now dive
Into the unexplored deeps of me--
Delve and bring up and give
All that is submerged, encased, unfolded,
That is yet the best.

ART AND LIFE

When Art goes bounding, lean,
Up hill-tops fired green
To pluck a rose for life.

Life like a broody hen
Cluck-clucks him back again.

But when Art, imbecile,
Sits old and chill
On sidings shaven clean,
And counts his clustering
Dead daisies on a string
With witless laughter....

Then like a new Jill
Toiling up a hill
Life scrambles after.

BROOKLYN BRIDGE

Pythoness body--arching
Over the night like an ecstasy--
I feel your coils tightening...
And the world's lessening breath.

DREAMS

Men die...
Dreams only change their houses.
They cannot be lined up against a wall
And quietly buried under ground,
And no more heard of...
However deep the pit and heaped the clay--
Like seedlings of old time
Hooding a sacred rose under the ice cap of the world--
Dreams will to light.

THE FIRE

The old men of the world have made a fire
To warm their trembling hands.
They poke the young men in.
The young men burn like withes.

If one run a little way,
The old men are wrath.
They catch him and bind him and throw him again to the flames.
Green withes burn slow...
And the smoke of the young men's torment
Rises round and sheer as the trunk of a pillared oak,
And the darkness thereof spreads over the sky....

Green withes burn slow...
And the old men of the world sit round the fire
And rub their hands....
But the smoke of the young men's torment
Ascends up for ever and ever.

A MEMORY

I remember
The crackle of the palm trees
Over the mooned white roofs of the town...
The shining town...
And the tender fumbling of the surf
On the sulphur-yellow beaches
As we sat... a little apart... in the close-pressing night.

The moon hung above us like a golden mango,
And the moist air clung to our faces,
Warm and fragrant as the open mouth of a child
And we watched the out-flung sea
Rolling to the purple edge of the world,
Yet ever back upon itself...
As we...

Inadequate night...
And mooned white memory
Of a tropic sea...
How softly it comes up
Like an ungathered lily.

THE EDGE

I thought to die that night in the solitude where they would never find me...
But there was time...
And I lay quietly on the drawn knees of the mountain,
 staring into the abyss...
I do not know how long...
I could not count the hours, they ran so fast
Like little bare-foot urchins--shaking my hands away...
But I remember
Somewhere water trickled like a thin severed vein...
And a wind came out of the grass,
Touching me gently, tentatively, like a paw.

As the night grew
The gray cloud that had covered the sky like sackcloth
Fell in ashen folds about the hills,

Like hooded virgins, pulling their cloaks about them...
There must have been a spent moon,
For the Tall One's veil held a shimmer of silver...

That too I remember...
And the tenderly rocking mountain
Silence
And beating stars...

Dawn
Lay like a waxen hand upon the world,
And folded hills
Broke into a sudden wonder of peaks, stemming clear and cold,
Till the Tall One bloomed like a lily,
Flecked with sun,
Fine as a golden pollen--
It seemed a wind might blow it from the snow.

I smelled the raw sweet essences of things,
And heard spiders in the leaves
And ticking of little feet,
As tiny creatures came out of their doors
To see God pouring light into his star...

... It seemed life held
No future and no past but this...

And I too got up stiffly from the earth,
And held my heart up like a cup...

THE GARDEN

Bountiful Givers,
I look along the years
And see the flowers you threw...
Anemones
And sprigs of gray
Sparse heather of the rocks,
Or a wild violet
Or daisy of a daisied field...
But each your best.

I might have worn them on my breast
To wilt in the long day...
I might have stemmed them in a narrow vase
And watched each petal sallowing...
I might have held them so--mechanically--
Till the wind winnowed all the leaves
And left upon my hands
A little smear of dust.
Instead
I hid them in the soft warm loam
Of a dim shadowed place...
Deep
In a still cool grotto,
Lit only by the memories of stars
And the wide and luminous eyes
Of dead poets
That love me and that I love...
Deep... deep...
Where none may see--not even ye who gave--
About my soul your garden beautiful.

UNDER-SONG

There is music in the strong
 Deep-throated bush,
Whisperings of song
 Heard in the leaves' hush--
Ballads of the trees
 In tongues unknown--
A reminiscent tone
 On minor keys...

Boughs swaying to and fro
 Though no winds pass...
Faint odors in the grass
 Where no flowers grow,
And flutterings of wings
 And faint first notes,
Once babbled on the boughs
 Of faded springs.

Is it music from the graves
 Of all things fair
Trembling on the staves
 Of spacious air--
Fluted by the winds
 Songs with no words--
Sonatas from the throats
 Of master birds?

One peering through the husk
 Of darkness thrown
May hear it in the dusk--

That ancient tone,
Silvery as the light
 Of long dead stars
Yet falling through the night
 In trembling bars.

A WORN ROSE

Where to-day would a dainty buyer
Imbibe your scented juice,
Pale ruin with a heart of fire;
Drain your succulence with her lips,
Grown sapless from much use...
Make minister of her desire
A chalice cup where no bee sips--
 Where no wasp wanders in?

Close to her white flesh housed an hour,
 One held you... her spent form
Drew on yours for its wasted dower--
What favour could she do you more?
 Yet, of all who drink therein,
 None know it is the warm
Odorous heart of a ravished flower
Tingles so in her mouth's red core...

IRON WINE

The ore in the crucible is pungent, smelling like acrid wine,
It is dusky red, like the ebb of poppies,
And purple, like the blood of elderberries.
Surely it is a strong wine--juice distilled of the fierce iron.
I am drunk of its fumes.
I feel its fiery flux
Diffusing, permeating,
Working some strange alchemy...
So that I turn aside from the goodly board,
So that I look askance upon the common cup,
And from the mouths of crucibles
Suck forth the acrid sap.

DISPOSSESSED

Tender and tremulous green of leaves
Turned up by the wind,
Twanging among the vines--
Wind in the grass
Blowing a clear path
For the new-stripped soul to pass...

The naked soul in the sunlight...
Like a wisp of smoke in the sunlight
On the hill-side shimmering.

Dance light on the wind, little soul,

Like a thistle-down floating
Over the butterflies
And the lumbering bees...

Come away from that tree
And its shadow grey as a stone...

Bathe in the pools of light
On the hillside shimmering--
Shining and wetted and warm in the sun-spray falling like golden rain--

But do not linger and look
At that bleak thing under the tree.

THE STAR

Last night
I watched a star fall like a great pearl into the sea,
Till my ego expanding encompassed sea and star,
Containing both as in a trembling cup.

THE TIDINGS

(Easter 1916)

Censored lies that mimic truth...
 Censored truth as pale as fear...
My heart is like a rousing bell--
 And but the dead to hear...

My heart is like a mother bird,
 Circling ever higher,
And the nest-tree rimmed about
 By a forest fire...

My heart is like a lover foiled
 By a broken stair--
They are fighting to-night in Sackville Street,
 And I am not there!

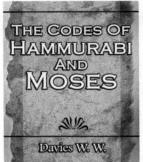

The Codes Of Hammurabi And Moses
W. W. Davies

QTY

The discovery of the Hammurabi Code is one of the greatest achievements of archaeology, and is of paramount interest, not only to the student of the Bible, but also to all those interested in ancient history...

Religion   **ISBN:** *1-59462-338-4*   **Pages:132**
MSRP *$12.95*

The Theory of Moral Sentiments
Adam Smith

QTY

This work from 1749. contains original theories of conscience amd moral judgment and it is the foundation for systemof morals.

Philosophy   **ISBN:** *1-59462-777-0*   **Pages:536**
MSRP *$19.95*

Jessica's First Prayer
Hesba Stretton

QTY

In a screened and secluded corner of one of the many railway-bridges which span the streets of London there could be seen a few years ago, from five o'clock every morning until half past eight, a tidily set-out coffee-stall, consisting of a trestle and board, upon which stood two large tin cans, with a small fire of charcoal burning under each so as to keep the coffee boiling during the early hours of the morning when the work-people were thronging into the city on their way to their daily toil...

Childrens   **ISBN:** *1-59462-373-2*   **Pages:84**
MSRP *$9.95*

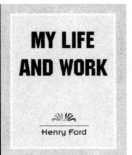

My Life and Work
Henry Ford

QTY

Henry Ford revolutionized the world with his implementation of mass production for the Model T automobile. Gain valuable business insight into his life and work with his own auto-biography... "We have only started on our development of our country we have not as yet, with all our talk of wonderful progress, done more than scratch the surface. The progress has been wonderful enough but..."

Biographies/   **ISBN:** *1-59462-198-5*   **Pages:300**
MSRP *$21.95*

The Art of Cross-Examination
Francis Wellman

QTY

I presume it is the experience of every author, after his first book is published upon an important subject, to be almost overwhelmed with a wealth of ideas and illustrations which could readily have been included in his book, and which to his own mind, at least, seem to make a second edition inevitable. Such certainly was the case with me; and when the first edition had reached its sixth impression in five months, I rejoiced to learn that it seemed to my publishers that the book had met with a sufficiently favorable reception to justify a second and considerably enlarged edition. ..

Pages:412

Reference   ISBN: *1-59462-647-2*   MSRP *$19.95*

On the Duty of Civil Disobedience
Henry David Thoreau

QTY

Thoreau wrote his famous essay, On the Duty of Civil Disobedience, as a protest against an unjust but popular war and the immoral but popular institution of slave-owning. He did more than write—he declined to pay his taxes, and was hauled off to gaol in consequence. Who can say how much this refusal of his hastened the end of the war and of slavery ?

Law   ISBN: *1-59462-747-9*   **Pages:48**

MSRP *$7.45*

Dream Psychology Psychoanalysis for Beginners
Sigmund Freud

QTY

Sigmund Freud, born Sigismund Schlomo Freud (May 6, 1856 - September 23, 1939), was a Jewish-Austrian neurologist and psychiatrist who co-founded the psychoanalytic school of psychology. Freud is best known for his theories of the unconscious mind, especially involving the mechanism of repression; his redefinition of sexual desire as mobile and directed towards a wide variety of objects; and his therapeutic techniques, especially his understanding of transference in the therapeutic relationship and the presumed value of dreams as sources of insight into unconscious desires.

Dream Psychology
Psychoanalysis for Beginners

Sigmund Freud

Pages:196

Psychology   ISBN: *1-59462-905-6*   MSRP *$15.45*

The Miracle of Right Thought
Orison Swett Marden

QTY

Believe with all of your heart that you will do what you were made to do. When the mind has once formed the habit of holding cheerful, happy, prosperous pictures, it will not be easy to form the opposite habit. It does not matter how improbable or how far away this realization may see, or how dark the prospects may be, if we visualize them as best we can, as vividly as possible, hold tenaciously to them and vigorously struggle to attain them, they will gradually become actualized, realized in the life. But a desire, a longing without endeavor, a yearning abandoned or held indifferently will vanish without realization.

Pages:360

Self Help   ISBN: *1-59462-644-8*   MSRP *$25.45*

QTY

☐ **The Rosicrucian Cosmo-Conception Mystic Christianity** *by Max Heindel* ISBN: *1-59462-188-8* **$38.95**
The Rosicrucian Cosmo-conception is not dogmatic, neither does it appeal to any other authority than the reason of the student. It is: not controversial, but is: sent forth in the, hope that it may help to clear... New Age/Religion Pages 646

☐ **Abandonment To Divine Providence** *by Jean-Pierre de Caussade* ISBN: *1-59462-228-0* **$25.95**
"The Rev. Jean Pierre de Caussade was one of the most remarkable spiritual writers of the Society of Jesus in France in the 18th Century. His death took place at Toulouse in 1751. His works have gone through many editions and have been republished... Inspirational/Religion Pages 400

☐ **Mental Chemistry** *by Charles Haanel* ISBN: *1-59462-192-6* **$23.95**
Mental Chemistry allows the change of material conditions by combining and appropriately utilizing the power of the mind. Much like applied chemistry creates something new and unique out of careful combinations of chemicals the mastery of mental chemistry... New Age Pages 354

☐ **The Letters of Robert Browning and Elizabeth Barret Barrett 1845-1846 vol II** ISBN: *1-59462-193-4* **$35.95**
by Robert Browning and Elizabeth Barrett Biographies Pages 596

☐ **Gleanings In Genesis (volume I)** *by Arthur W. Pink* ISBN: *1-59462-130-6* **$27.45**
Appropriately has Genesis been termed "the seed plot of the Bible" for in it we have, in germ form, almost all of the great doctrines which are afterwards fully developed in the books of Scripture which follow... Religion/Inspirational Pages 420

☐ **The Master Key** *by L. W. de Laurence* ISBN: *1-59462-001-6* **$30.95**
In no branch of human knowledge has there been a more lively increase of the spirit of research during the past few years than in the study of Psychology, Concentration and Mental Discipline. The requests for authentic lessons in Thought Control, Mental Discipline and... New Age/Business Pages 422

☐ **The Lesser Key Of Solomon Goetia** *by L. W. de Laurence* ISBN: *1-59462-092-X* **$9.95**
This translation of the first book of the "Lernegton" which is now for the first time made accessible to students of Talismanic Magic was done, after careful collation and edition, from numerous Ancient Manuscripts in Hebrew, Latin, and French... New Age/Occult Pages 92

☐ **Rubaiyat Of Omar Khayyam** *by Edward Fitzgerald* ISBN:*1-59462-332-5* **$13.95**
Edward Fitzgerald, whom the world has already learned, in spite of his own efforts to remain within the shadow of anonymity, to look upon as one of the rarest poets of the century, was born at Bredfield, in Suffolk, on the 31st of March, 1809. He was the third son of John Purcell... Music Pages 172

☐ **Ancient Law** *by Henry Maine* ISBN: *1-59462-128-4* **$29.95**
The chief object of the following pages is to indicate some of the earliest ideas of mankind, as they are reflected in Ancient Law, and to point out the relation of those ideas to modern thought. Religiom/History Pages 452

☐ **Far-Away Stories** *by William J. Locke* ISBN: *1-59462-129-2* **$19.45**
"Good wine needs no bush, but a collection of mixed vintages does. And this book is just such a collection. Some of the stories I do not want to remain buried for ever in the museum files of dead magazine-numbers an author's not unpardonable vanity..." Fiction Pages 272

☐ **Life of David Crockett** *by David Crockett* ISBN: *1-59462-250-7* **$27.45**
"Colonel David Crockett was one of the most remarkable men of the times in which he lived. Born in humble life, but gifted with a strong will, an indomitable courage, and unremitting perseverance... Biographies/New Age Pages 424

☐ **Lip-Reading** *by Edward Nitchie* ISBN: *1-59462-206-X* **$25.95**
Edward B. Nitchie, founder of the New York School for the Hard of Hearing, now the Nitchie School of Lip-Reading, Inc, wrote "LIP-READING Principles and Practice". The development and perfecting of this meritorious work on lip-reading was an undertaking... How-to Pages 400

☐ **A Handbook of Suggestive Therapeutics, Applied Hypnotism, Psychic Science** ISBN: *1-59462-214-0* **$24.95**
by Henry Munro Health/New Age/Health/Self-help Pages 376

☐ **A Doll's House: and Two Other Plays** *by Henrik Ibsen* ISBN: *1-59462-112-8* **$19.95**
Henrik Ibsen created this classic when in revolutionary 1848 Rome. Introducing some striking concepts in playwriting for the realist genre, this play has been studied the world over. Fiction/Classics/Plays 308

☐ **The Light of Asia** *by sir Edwin Arnold* ISBN: *1-59462-204-3* **$13.95**
In this poetic masterpiece, Edwin Arnold describes the life and teachings of Buddha. The man who was to become known as Buddha to the world was born as Prince Gautama of India but he rejected the worldly riches and abandoned the reigns of power when... Religion/History/Biographies Pages 170

☐ **The Complete Works of Guy de Maupassant** *by Guy de Maupassant* ISBN: *1-59462-157-8* **$16.95**
"For days and days, nights and nights, I had dreamed of that first kiss which was to consecrate our engagement, and I knew not on what spot I should put my lips..." Fiction/Classics Pages 240

☐ **The Art of Cross-Examination** *by Francis L. Wellman* ISBN: *1-59462-309-0* **$26.95**
Written by a renowned trial lawyer, Wellman imparts his experience and uses case studies to explain how to use psychology to extract desired information through questioning. How-to/Science/Reference Pages 408

☐ **Answered or Unanswered?** *by Louisa Vaughan* ISBN: *1-59462-248-5* **$10.95**
Miracles of Faith in China Religion Pages 112

☐ **The Edinburgh Lectures on Mental Science (1909)** *by Thomas* ISBN: *1-59462-008-3* **$11.95**
This book contains the substance of a course of lectures recently given by the writer in the Queen Street Hail, Edinburgh. Its purpose is to indicate the Natural Principles governing the relation between Mental Action and Material Conditions... New Age/Psychology Pages 148

☐ **Ayesha** *by H. Rider Haggard* ISBN: *1-59462-301-5* **$24.95**
Verily and indeed it is the unexpected that happens! Probably if there was one person upon the earth from whom the Editor of this, and of a certain previous history, did not expect to hear again... Classics Pages 380

☐ **Ayala's Angel** *by Anthony Trollope* ISBN: *1-59462-352-X* **$29.95**
The two girls were both pretty, but Lucy who was twenty-one who supposed to be simple and comparatively unattractive, whereas Ayala was credited, as her Bombwhat romantic name might show, with poetic charm and a taste for romance. Ayala when her father died was nineteen... Fiction Pages 484

☐ **The American Commonwealth** *by James Bryce* ISBN: *1-59462-286-8* **$34.45**
An interpretation of American democratic political theory. It examines political mechanics and society from the perspective of Scotsman James Bryce Politics Pages 572

☐ **Stories of the Pilgrims** *by Margaret P. Pumphrey* ISBN: *1-59462-116-0* **$17.95**
This book explores pilgrims religious oppression in England as well as their escape to Holland and eventual crossing to America on the Mayflower, and their early days in New England... History Pages 268

QTY

The Fasting Cure *by Sinclair Upton*   ISBN: *1-59462-222-1* **$13.95**
In the Cosmopolitan Magazine for May, 1910, and in the Contemporary Review (London) for April, 1910, I published an article dealing with my experiences in fasting. I have written a great many magazine articles, but never one which attracted so much attention... New Age/Self Help/Health Pages 164

Hebrew Astrology *by Sepharial*   ISBN: *1-59462-308-2* **$13.45**
In these days of advanced thinking it is a matter of common observation that we have left many of the old landmarks behind and that we are now pressing forward to greater heights and to a wider horizon than that which represented the mind-content of our progenitors...   Astrology Pages 144

Thought Vibration or The Law of Attraction in the Thought World   ISBN: *1-59462-127-6* **$12.95**
by William Walker Atkinson   Psychology/Religion Pages 144

Optimism *by Helen Keller*   ISBN: *1-59462-108-X* **$15.95**
Helen Keller was blind, deaf, and mute since 19 months old, yet famously learned how to overcome these handicaps, communicate with the world, and spread her lectures promoting optimism. An inspiring read for everyone...   Biographies/Inspirational Pages 84

Sara Crewe *by Frances Burnett*   ISBN: *1-59462-360-0* **$9.45**
In the first place, Miss Minchin lived in London. Her home was a large, dull, tall one, in a large, dull square, where all the houses were alike, and all the sparrows were alike, and where all the door-knockers made the same heavy sound...   Childrens/Classic Pages 88

The Autobiography of Benjamin Franklin *by Benjamin Franklin*   ISBN: *1-59462-135-7* **$24.95**
The Autobiography of Benjamin Franklin has probably been more extensively read than any other American historical work, and no other book of its kind has had such ups and downs of fortune. Franklin lived for many years in England, where he was agent...   Biographies/History Pages 332

Name	
Email	
Telephone	
Address	
City, State ZIP	

☐ **Credit Card**   ☐ **Check / Money Order**

Credit Card Number	
Expiration Date	
Signature	

Please Mail to: Book Jungle
PO Box 2226
Champaign, IL 61825
or Fax to: 630-214-0564

ORDERING INFORMATION

web: *www.bookjungle.com*
email: *sales@bookjungle.com*
fax: *630-214-0564*
mail: *Book Jungle PO Box 2226 Champaign, IL 61825*
or PayPal *to sales@bookjungle.com*

Please contact us for bulk discounts

DIRECT-ORDER TERMS

**20% Discount if You Order
Two or More Books**
Free Domestic Shipping!
Accepted: Master Card, Visa,
Discover, American Express

Lightning Source UK Ltd.
Milton Keynes UK
UKHW031911080620
364669UK00006B/1273

9 781438 595238